Jordan Blake

Tools For Digital Marketing

"Dedicated to the relentless pursuit of mastery, to the marketers who thrive on innovation, and to the entrepreneurs who dare to redefine the status quo. May 'Mastering Modern Marketing' be your compass on this exhilarating journey." - Jordan Blake

"In the symphony of modern marketing, each note resonates with innovation, strategy, and the pulse of the digital era. 'Mastering Modern Marketing' is your conductor's baton—guiding you to orchestrate success in the ever-evolving landscape." -

Jordan Blake

Contents

1.

2.

3.

4.

5.

6.

7.

8.

9.

10.

11.

12.

13.

14.

15.

16.

17.

18.

19.

20.

21.

22.

Foreword

Foreword

In the labyrinth of modern marketing, where trends emerge with the velocity of a social media share and strategies pivot like a viral meme, the need for guidance becomes paramount. As we stand at the threshold of "Mastering Modern Marketing," I find great pleasure in introducing this navigational compass for the savvy marketer and the ambitious entrepreneur alike.

This comprehensive guide, curated with precision and passion, is not merely a collection of strategies; it is a testament to the dynamic nature of an industry that refuses to stand still. In these pages, we embark on a journey of discovery, where every chapter is a stepping stone toward mastery. From the intricacies of the latest tools to the artistry of crafting a compelling narrative in the digital age, the insights within are as diverse as the facets of modern marketing itself.

As the marketing landscape continues to evolve, so too does the demand for adaptability and innovation. "Mastering Modern Marketing" isn't just a book; it's a dynamic companion designed to keep you ahead of the curve. Whether you're diving into the depths of analytics or scaling the heights of creative brilliance, this guide offers a roadmap, equipping you to navigate the challenges and capitalize on the opportunities that lie ahead.

Through years of immersion in this ever-evolving field, I've witnessed the transformative power of staying ahead of the trends. It is my sincere hope that this guide becomes a source of inspiration, knowledge, and actionable insights for all those who seek to not only understand the intricacies of modern marketing but to master them.

So, with excitement and anticipation, I invite you to turn the pages, embrace the insights, and embark on your journey to "Mastering Modern Marketing."

Jordan   Blake

Preface

In the ever-shifting landscape of modern marketing, where algorithms dance, and consumer behaviors waltz to an ever-changing tune, the pursuit of mastery becomes both an art and a science. As we embark on this journey together, "Mastering Modern Marketing," I invite you to delve into a world where creativity meets analytics, and innovation harmonizes with strategy.

In these pages, we explore the intricate tapestry of the latest tools and strategies that define contemporary marketing. From the algorithms that weave the digital fabric to the strategies that resonate with today's dynamic audience, this guide is a compass through the uncharted territories of the marketing realm.

Drawing on my years of experience navigating this ever-evolving landscape, I've crafted insights, observations, and actionable techniques to empower you on your quest for mastery. Whether you're a seasoned marketer seeking fresh perspectives or an aspiring entrepreneur ready to embark on your digital journey, this guide is a beacon, guiding you through the complexities and illuminating the pathways to success.

Together, let's unlock the secrets of successful modern marketing—where creativity, strategy, and innovation converge. May this guide inspire your journey and equip you with the tools to not only keep pace with the trends but to dance ahead, setting the rhythm for your success. Welcome to "Mastering Modern Marketing." Let the journey begin.

Jordan   Blake

Acknowledgement

Acknowledgments

Embarking on the journey of creating "Mastering Modern Marketing" has been a rewarding odyssey, and I am deeply grateful for the collective efforts and support that have brought this endeavor to fruition.

To the tireless contributors, whose expertise and insights have enriched the pages of this guide, I extend my heartfelt appreciation. Your passion for the ever-evolving world of marketing has illuminated the path for readers seeking mastery in this dynamic realm.

A sincere thank you to the team behind the scenes—editors, designers, and collaborators—who have worked diligently to transform ideas into a tangible guide. Your dedication to excellence is evident on every page.

To the mentors and industry leaders whose wisdom has shaped my understanding of marketing, I express my gratitude. Your guidance has been invaluable, and this guide stands as a tribute to the collective knowledge shared within our community.

To the readers, enthusiasts, and professionals who seek to master the art and science of modern marketing, thank you for allowing this guide to be a part of your journey. May the insights within these pages empower and inspire you to achieve new heights in your endeavors.

With gratitude,

Jordan   Blake

1

Google Analytics

To use Google Analytics:

1. Sign Up: Create a Google Analytics account or use an existing Google account to sign in.

2. Set Up Property: Add a new property for your website. Obtain the tracking code provided.

3. Install Tracking Code: Paste the tracking code into the header of your website's HTML. This allows Google Analytics to collect data.

4. Verify Tracking: Confirm the tracking code is working by checking the real-time data in Google Analytics.

5. Configure Goals: Define specific goals (e.g., conversions, sign-ups) to track user interactions.

6. Explore Reports: Navigate through various reports in Google Analytics to analyze user demographics, behavior, traffic sources, and more.

7. Create Custom Reports: Tailor reports based on your marketing objectives.

8. Set Up Alerts: Receive notifications for significant changes in website metrics.

9. Use UTM Parameters: Implement UTM parameters in your URLs to track campaign-specific data.

10. Review E-commerce Data (if applicable): For online stores, set up e-commerce tracking to analyze sales performance.

By leveraging these features, you can gain valuable insights into your website's performance and optimize your digital marketing efforts accordingly.

2

Google Ads:

To use Google Ads:

1. Create an Account: Sign up for a Google Ads account using your Google account.

2. Define Campaign Goals: Determine the objectives of your advertising campaign, such as website traffic, leads, or sales.

3. Set Budget and Bidding: Establish a daily or campaign budget, and choose a bidding strategy that aligns with your goals.

4.Target Audience: Define your target audience based on demographics, interests, and behavior.

5. Create Ad Groups: Organize your ads into relevant ad groups, each focusing on specific keywords or themes.

6. Keyword Research: Conduct keyword research to identify relevant and high-performing keywords for your ads.

7. Create Compelling Ads: Craft engaging ad copy with a clear call-to-action. Use appealing visuals if applicable.

8. Choose Ad Extensions: Enhance your ads with extensions like site links, callouts, and location information.

9. Set Up Conversion Tracking: Implement conversion tracking to measure the success of your campaigns in terms of desired actions.

10. Launch Campaign: Review your settings and launch your Google Ads campaign.

11. Monitor Performance: Regularly check your campaign performance through the Google Ads dashboard.

12. Optimize Ads: Adjust your ads, keywords, and targeting based on performance data to improve results.

13. A/B Testing: Experiment with different ad variations to identify the most effective elements.

14. Utilize Ad Schedule: Schedule ads to appear at specific times when your target audience is most active.

15. Explore Additional Campaign Types: Google Ads offers various campaign types, including search, display, video, and more. Explore options based on your marketing objectives.

By following these steps, you can effectively set up and manage Google Ads campaigns to reach your advertising goals.

3

Facebook Ads Manager:

To use Facebook Ads Manager:

1. Access Ads Manager: Log in to your Facebook account and navigate to Ads Manager.

2. Create Ad Account: If you don't have an ad account, create one. Otherwise, use an existing ad account.

3. Choose Ad Objective: Select the objective that aligns with your campaign goals, such as awareness, consideration, or conversion.

4.Define Target Audience: Specify your target audience based on demographics, interests, and behaviors.

5. Set Budget and Schedule: Determine your daily or lifetime budget and choose the ad schedule for when your ads will run.

6. Select Ad Placements: Choose where your ads will appear, whether in Facebook feeds, Instagram, Audience Network, or other placements.

7. Create Ad Creative: Develop engaging ad content, including images, videos, ad copy, and a call-to-action.

8. Add Ad Formats: Choose ad formats such as carousel, single image, slideshow, or video, depending on your campaign goals.

9. Set Bidding Strategy: Decide on a bidding strategy, like automatic bidding or manual bidding.

10. Review Ad Preview: Preview your ad to ensure it looks appealing and functions correctly.

11. Add Tracking: Implement Facebook Pixel on your website for tracking conversions and optimizing ad delivery.

12. Place Order: Once satisfied, place your ad order.

13. Monitor Performance: Regularly check the performance metrics in Ads Manager to assess the effectiveness of your campaigns.

14. Optimize Ads: Adjust your targeting, creative elements, and budget based on performance data.

15. A/B Testing: Experiment with different ad variations to identify the most effective elements.

By following these steps, you can effectively utilize Facebook Ads Manager to create and manage targeted advertising campaigns on Facebook and Instagram.

4

Mailchimp for email marketing:

To use Mailchimp for email marketing:

1. Create an Account: Sign up for a Mailchimp account.

2. Set Up Your Audience: Create a mailing list or import existing contacts into Mailchimp.

3. Design Your Campaign: Choose the type of campaign you want to create (e.g., email, automation), and use Mailchimp's drag-and-drop editor to design your email.

4. Add Content: Craft compelling email content, including text, images, and links. Ensure a clear call-to-action.

5. Personalization: Personalize your emails by addressing recipients by name and tailoring content based on their preferences.

6. Choose Recipients: Select the audience or segment you want to target with your email campaign.

7. Set Sending Time: Schedule the delivery time for your email campaign to optimize open rates.

8. Preview and Test: Preview your email to ensure it looks good on different devices. Send test emails to check formatting and links.

9. Review and Confirm: Double-check all elements of your campaign and confirm before sending.

10. Monitor Campaign Analytics: Track key metrics such as open rates, click-through rates, and conversions using Mailchimp's analytics tools.

11. Automate Campaigns: Explore Mailchimp's automation features for setting up automated email sequences based on user behavior.

12. Integrate with Other Tools: Connect Mailchimp with other tools, like your website or e-commerce platform, for seamless data sharing.

13. Segmentation: Utilize audience segmentation to send targeted messages to specific groups within your mailing list.

14. Manage Unsubscribes and Bounces: Monitor and manage unsubscribes and email bounces to maintain a healthy email list.

15. Stay Compliant: Adhere to email marketing regulations and best practices to avoid potential issues.

By following these steps, you can effectively use Mailchimp to create, send, and analyze the performance of your email marketing campaigns.

5

HubSpot

To use HubSpot:

1. Create an Account: Sign up for a HubSpot account.

2. Set Up Your Dashboard: Customize your dashboard to display key metrics and tools relevant to your marketing, sales, and customer service needs.

3. Import Contacts: Import your contacts into HubSpot or integrate with other platforms to centralize your customer data.

4. Create Lists and Segments: Organize your contacts by creating lists and segments based on criteria like demographics, behavior, or engagement.

5. Content Creation: Use HubSpot's content creation tools to develop blog posts, landing pages, and other marketing collateral.

6. Email Marketing: Leverage HubSpot for email marketing by creating and sending personalized email campaigns.

7. Lead Capture Forms: Design and implement lead capture forms on your website to gather information from visitors.

8. Sales Automation: Explore sales automation features to streamline your sales processes, including lead scoring and task automation.

9. CRM Integration: Integrate HubSpot's CRM to manage customer relationships, track deals, and monitor sales performance.

10. Social Media Publishing: Schedule and publish social media posts directly from HubSpot, and monitor social interactions.

11. Analytics: Utilize HubSpot's analytics tools to track the performance of your marketing efforts, from website visits to lead conversions.

12. Marketing Automation: Set up automated workflows to nurture leads and guide them through the marketing funnel.

13. Live Chat: Implement live chat on your website for real-time customer engagement.

14. Customer Service: Use HubSpot's customer service tools to manage tickets, provide support, and track customer satisfaction.

15. Reports and Dashboards: Generate reports and customize dashboards to gain insights into your marketing, sales, and service performance.

By incorporating these features, you can effectively use HubSpot as an integrated platform for marketing, sales, and customer service activities.

6

Hootsuite for social media management:

To use Hootsuite for social media management:

1. Create an Account: Sign up for a Hootsuite account.

2. Connect Social Media Accounts: Add and connect your social media accounts (e.g., Facebook, Twitter, Instagram) to Hootsuite.

3. Set Up Streams: Create customized streams to monitor your social media feeds, mentions, and relevant hashtags in one place.

4. Schedule Posts: Use the scheduling feature to plan and schedule posts across multiple social media platforms.

5. Content Calendar: Utilize the content calendar to visualize and manage your social media posting schedule.

6. Social Listening: Monitor conversations and trends relevant to your brand using Hootsuite's social listening tools.

7. Analytics: Track and analyze social media performance with Hootsuite's analytics, including engagement, reach, and follower growth.

8. Team Collaboration: Collaborate with team members by assigning tasks, responding to comments, and managing social media activities collaboratively.

9. Automated Posting: Set up automated posting for specific times, allowing Hootsuite to publish content on your behalf.

10. RSS Feeds: Integrate RSS feeds to discover and share relevant content from trusted sources within your industry.

11. Bulk Scheduling: Save time by scheduling multiple posts at once using Hootsuite's bulk scheduling feature.

12. Mobile App: Stay connected on the go by using Hootsuite's mobile app to manage your social media from your smartphone.

13. Ad Campaign Management: Manage and track social media advertising campaigns directly from Hootsuite.

14. Security Features: Utilize security features to manage access levels and permissions for team members.

15. Education and Certification:.Take advantage of Hootsuite's educational resources and certifications to enhance your social media management skills.

By incorporating these functionalities, you can efficiently use Hootsuite to streamline and optimize your social media management efforts.

7

Buffer for social media scheduling:

To use Buffer for social media scheduling:

1. Create an Account: Sign up for a Buffer account.

2. Connect Social Media Accounts: Add and connect your social media accounts, such as Facebook, Twitter, LinkedIn, or Instagram, to Buffer.

3. Set Posting Schedule: Define your posting schedule by specifying the days and times you want to share content on each platform.

4. Install Browser Extension (Optional): Use the Buffer browser extension to easily add content to your queue while browsing the web.

5. Compose and Schedule Posts: Create social media posts with text, images, or links. Schedule posts for specific times or add them to your queue for automatic scheduling.

6. View and Edit Queue: Monitor your content queue to see the upcoming posts. Edit, rearrange, or reschedule posts as needed.

7. Collaborate with Team Members (if applicable): If you're working with a team, collaborate by assigning tasks and roles within Buffer.

8. Analytics: Track post performance using Buffer's analytics to understand engagement, clicks, and other key metrics.

9. Respond to Comments and Mentions: Engage with your audience by responding to comments and mentions directly within Buffer.

10. Repost and Requeue: Easily repost or requeue evergreen content for continued visibility.

11. Customize Post Formats: Tailor posts for each platform by adjusting post formats, hashtags, or emojis.

12. Use Buffer for Instagram: Leverage Buffer's features for scheduling and posting content on Instagram, including carousel posts.

13. Integration with Canva (Optional): If using Canva, integrate it with Buffer to design and schedule visually appealing posts.

14. Mobile App: Stay connected on the go with the Buffer mobile app to manage and monitor your social media posts.

15. Educational Resources: Explore Buffer's educational resources to enhance your social media strategy and skills.

By following these steps, you can effectively use Buffer to schedule, manage, and analyze your social media posts across various platforms.

8

SEO tools such as SEMrush or Moz for optimizing your website:

To use SEO tools such as SEMrush or Moz for optimizing your website:

1. Sign Up/Log In: Create an account on the chosen SEO tool's website or log in if you already have an account.

2. Add Your Website: Input your website's URL into the tool to start analyzing its performance.

3. Site Audit: Conduct a site audit to identify and address on-page SEO issues, including broken links, missing meta tags, and other technical issues.

4. Keyword Research: Use the tool to perform keyword research to discover relevant keywords for your content and identify their search volume and competition.

5. Competitor Analysis: Analyze your competitors' websites to understand their strategies, keywords, and backlink profiles.

6. Backlink Analysis: Examine your website's backlink profile and identify opportunities for acquiring high-quality backlinks.

7. Rank Tracking: Monitor your website's rankings for specific keywords over time.

8. On-Page SEO Recommendations: Implement on-page SEO recommendations provided by the tool to optimize your content for search engines.

9. Content Gap Analysis: Identify content gaps in your industry and create new content to fill those gaps.

10. Local SEO (if applicable): Optimize your website for local search if you have a local business. Ensure accurate business information on platforms like Google My Business.

11. Technical SEO: Address technical issues such as site speed, mobile-friendliness, and schema markup to enhance user experience and search engine visibility.

12. Social Media Integration (if applicable): Some SEO tools provide insights into social media performance; integrate them to get a comprehensive view.

13. SEO Reporting: Generate and review reports to track the progress of your SEO efforts over time.

14. Educational Resources: Explore the educational materials provided by the SEO tool to stay informed about best practices and industry trends.

15. Integration with Other Tools: Integrate your SEO tool with other marketing tools for a unified analytics and reporting experience.

By incorporating these steps, you can leverage SEO tools to enhance your website's visibility, keyword rankings, and overall search engine performance.

9

Canva for designing graphics, presentations, and social media visuals:

To use Canva for designing graphics, presentations, and social media visuals:

1. Sign Up/Log In: Create a Canva account or log in if you already have one.

2. Choose a Design Type: Select the type of design you want to create, such as a social media post, presentation, poster, or custom dimensions.

3. Select a Template: Browse through Canva's extensive template library and choose a template that suits your design needs.

4. Customize Elements: Modify text, colors, images, and other elements in the template to match your brand or vision.

5. Add or Upload Images: Insert images from Canva's library or upload your own photos and graphics.

6. Use Canva Elements: Enhance your design with Canva's elements, including icons, illustrations, and shapes.

7. Text Editing: Customize text by choosing different fonts, sizes, and styles. Adjust alignment and spacing as needed.

8. Backgrounds and Colors: Experiment with backgrounds and color schemes to create a visually appealing design.

9. Collaboration (if applicable): If working with a team, collaborate by sharing your design for feedback or allowing others to edit.

10. Download or Share: Once satisfied, download your design in your preferred format (JPEG, PNG, PDF) or share it directly from Canva.

11. Presentation Mode (if creating presentations): Use Canva's presentation mode to showcase your slides seamlessly.

12. Brand Kit (if applicable): Utilize Canva's Brand Kit to store and apply your brand colors, fonts, and logos consistently.

13. Resize for Different Platforms: Easily resize your design for various platforms like social media posts, stories, or banners.

14. Animate Elements (if applicable): Add subtle animations to elements in your design for dynamic presentations or social media content.

15. Educational Resources: Explore Canva's tutorials and design guides to enhance your graphic design skills.

By following these steps, you can effectively use Canva to create visually appealing graphics, presentations, and social media visuals, even if you're not a professional designer.

10

Hotjar for understanding user behavior on your website through heatmaps and analytics:

T o use Hotjar for understanding user behavior on your website through heatmaps and analytics:

1. Sign Up/Log In: Create a Hotjar account or log in if you already have one.

2. Add Your Website: Enter your website URL and follow the instructions to install the Hotjar tracking code on your site. This usually involves adding a snippet of code to your website's HTML.

3. Create a New Heatmap: Once the tracking code is installed, go to Hotjar and create a new heatmap for the specific page or pages you want to analyze.

4. Select Heatmap Type: Choose the type of heatmap you want to generate, such as click, move, or scroll heatmap.

5. Adjust Settings: Customize settings like the date range and device type to refine your heatmap analysis.

6. View Heatmap Results: After a sufficient amount of data is collected, view the heatmap results to visualize user interactions on your website.

7. Analyze Clicks: Identify which elements on your pages users click the most, helping you understand what attracts their attention.

8. Analyze Mouse Movements: Understand how users move their mouse across your pages, indicating areas of interest or confusion.

9. Analyze Scrolling Behavior: See how far users scroll down a page, providing insights into content engagement.

10. Review Form Analytics (if applicable): If you have forms on your website, use Hotjar to analyze form interactions and identify areas for improvement.

11. Session Recordings (if applicable): Explore Hotjar's session recording feature to watch individual user sessions and understand their behavior in more detail.

12. Feedback Polls (if applicable): Implement Hotjar's feedback polls to gather direct input from users about their experience.

13. Share Insights with Team (if applicable): If you're working in a team, share Hotjar insights to collectively understand and optimize user experience.

14. Identify Pain Points: Use Hotjar data to pinpoint potential issues or friction points in the user journey.

15. Continuous Monitoring: Regularly review Hotjar data to monitor changes in user behavior and make informed website optimizations.

By following these steps, you can effectively use Hotjar to gain valuable insights into how users interact with your website and make data-driven decisions to enhance their experience.

11

Trello for organizing and managing projects collaboratively:

To use Trello for organizing and managing projects collaboratively:

1. Create an Account/Log In: Sign up for a Trello account or log in if you already have one.

2. Create a Board: Start by creating a new board for your project. A board is a high-level container for your tasks and lists.

3. Create Lists: Within your board, create lists that represent different stages or categories of your project. For example, "To-Do," "In Progress," and "Completed."

4. Create Cards: Each task or item in your project is represented by a card. Create cards for specific tasks and place them in the appropriate lists.

5. Add Details to Cards: Open each card and add details such as due dates, checklists, attachments, labels, and descriptions.

6. Labels: Use labels to categorize or prioritize tasks. For example, you could use labels to identify tasks related to different team members or project components.

7. Checklists: Break down tasks into smaller, manageable steps using checklists within cards.

8. Attachments: Attach relevant files or links to cards for easy access to project-related resources.

9. Assign Members: Assign team members to specific tasks by adding them as members to cards. This helps clarify responsibilities.

10. Due Dates: Set due dates for tasks to keep the project on track and ensure timely completion.

11. Comments and Communication: Use comments to communicate with team members within cards. Mention team members to notify them directly.

12. Power-Ups (if applicable): Explore Trello's Power-Ups, which are additional features and integrations that enhance Trello's functionality.

13. Calendar View (if applicable): Switch to the calendar view to visualize due dates and project timelines.

14. Search and Filter: Use the search and filter options to quickly locate cards, lists, or boards.

15. Mobile App: Stay connected on the go by using the Trello mobile app for real-time updates and task management.

By following these steps, you can effectively use Trello to organize, collaborate, and manage projects with your team in a   visually   intuitive   way.

12

Buzzsumo for identifying popular content and influencers in your industry:

To use Buzzsumo for identifying popular content and influencers in your industry:

1. Sign Up/Log In: Create a Buzzsumo account or log in if you already have one.

2. Enter a Topic or Keyword: In the search bar, enter a relevant topic, keyword, or domain related to your industry.

3. Explore Top Content: View the top-performing content related to your query. Analyze the number of social media shares, backlinks, and overall engagement.

4. Filter Results: Utilize filters to refine your search based on content type, date range, language, and more.

5. Identify Influencers: Explore the "Influencers" tab to discover key influencers in your industry. Analyze their social media presence and the content they share.

6. Analyze Backlinks: Examine the backlinks of top-performing content to identify websites that are linking to popular articles. This can inform your link-building strategy.

7. Set Up Alerts (if applicable): Create content alerts to receive notifications when new content matching your criteria is published.

8. Content Analysis: Evaluate the content types that perform well, such as articles, videos, or infographics. Tailor your content strategy accordingly.

9. Competitor Analysis: Enter competitors' domains to see what content is working well for them. Identify opportunities to create similar or complementary content.

10. Export Data (if applicable): Export relevant data, such as top-performing content or influencer details, for further analysis or reporting.

11. Trending Now: Check the "Trending Now" section to discover real-time trends and popular topics in your industry.

12. Facebook Analyzer (if applicable): Use Buzzsumo's Facebook Analyzer to gain insights into Facebook engagement and performance.

13. Question Analyzer (if applicable): Explore questions related to your industry to understand what information your audience is seeking.

14. Collaboration (if applicable): If you're working in a team, collaborate by sharing insights and coordinating strategies based on Buzzsumo data.

15. Educational Resources: Take advantage of Buzzsumo's educational resources, including blog posts and guides, to enhance your content and influencer marketing strategies.

By following these steps, you can effectively use Buzzsumo to stay informed about popular content, identify influencers, and refine your content strategy based on industry trends.

13

Ahrefs for comprehensive SEO analysis, including backlink analysis and keyword research:

To use Ahrefs for comprehensive SEO analysis, including backlink analysis and keyword research:

1. Sign Up/Log In: Create an Ahrefs account or log in if you already have one.

2. Enter Your Domain: Enter your website's domain into the Ahrefs dashboard to initiate the analysis.

3. Site Explorer: Utilize the Site Explorer feature to gain an overview of your website's backlink profile, organic search traffic, and top-performing pages.

4. Backlink Analysis: Explore the "Backlinks" or "Referring Domains" section to view the websites linking to your content. Analyze the quality and quantity of backlinks.

5. Competitor Analysis: Enter competitor domains to compare backlink profiles and identify potential link-building opportunities.

6. Keyword Explorer: Use the Keyword Explorer tool to research relevant keywords for your industry. Analyze search volume, keyword difficulty, and click-through rates.

7. Content Gap Analysis: Identify content gaps by comparing your website's content with that of competitors. Discover topics you might be missing.

8. Rank Tracker: Set up the Rank Tracker to monitor your website's performance for specific keywords over time. Receive notifications of ranking changes.

9. Site Audit: Conduct a site audit to identify technical SEO issues such as broken links, duplicate content, and missing meta tags.

10. Content Explorer: Find popular content in your industry by using the Content Explorer. Analyze metrics like social shares and backlinks to understand content performance.

11. Keyword Rank Checker: Monitor the rankings of specific keywords to gauge your content's visibility in search results.

12. Top Pages: Identify your top-performing pages in terms of organic traffic, backlinks, and social shares.

13. Explore Featured Snippets (if applicable): Use Ahrefs to identify opportunities to capture featured snippets for specific keywords.

14. Set Up Alerts (if applicable): Receive alerts for new backlinks or changes in your website's performance using Ahrefs' alert features.

15. Educational Resources: Explore Ahrefs' educational resources, including blog posts and tutorials, to enhance your understanding of SEO strategies.

By following these steps, you can effectively use Ahrefs to conduct in-depth SEO analysis, improve your website's visibility, and refine your content and link-building strategies.

14

OptinMonster for creating and managing website pop-ups and opt-in forms:

To use OptinMonster for creating and managing website pop-ups and opt-in forms:

1. Sign Up/Log In: Create an OptinMonster account or log in if you already have one.

2. Create a New Campaign: Click on "Create Campaign" to start a new opt-in form or pop-up.

3. Choose a Campaign Type: Select the type of campaign you want to create, such as a lightbox popup, floating bar, slide-in, or inline form.

4. Select a Template: Choose a template that suits your design preferences and campaign goals.

5. Customize Design: Use the drag-and-drop builder to customize the design of your form or pop-up. Modify text, colors, images, and other elements.

6. Add Form Fields: Include the necessary form fields to collect the information you need from visitors.

7. Configure Display Rules: Set up display rules to determine when and where the campaign should appear. Define triggers like time delay, exit-intent, scroll percentage, or specific pages.

8. Integrate with Email Marketing Service: Connect OptinMonster with your email marketing service (e.g., Mailchimp, HubSpot) to seamlessly sync collected leads.

9. Advanced Targeting (if applicable): Utilize advanced targeting options to show campaigns based on user behavior, referral source, or other custom conditions.

10. A/B Testing: Set up A/B tests to experiment with different variations of your campaign and identify the most effective design or messaging.

11. Preview and Test: Preview your campaign to see how it will appear to visitors. Test the functionality to ensure a smooth user experience.

12. Publish Campaign: Once satisfied, publish your campaign to make it live on your website.

13. Analytics: Monitor campaign performance using OptinMonster's analytics. Track impressions, conversions, and conversion rates.

14. Retargeting Campaigns (if applicable): Explore retargeting campaigns to show specific messages to returning visitors or those who didn't convert initially.

15. Educational Resources: Take advantage of OptinMonster's guides and tutorials to optimize your lead generation strategy.

By following these steps, you can effectively use OptinMonster to create engaging and effective pop-ups and opt-in forms to capture leads and grow your email list.

15

Unbounce for building and optimizing landing pages for conversion:

To use Unbounce for building and optimizing landing pages for conversion:

1. Sign Up/Log In: Create an Unbounce account or log in if you already have one.

2. Create a New Landing Page: Click on "Create New" to start building a new landing page.

3. Choose a Template: Select a template from Unbounce's library that aligns with your campaign or create a new page from scratch.

4. Customize the Design: Use the drag-and-drop builder to customize the design of your landing page. Modify text, images, colors, and layout to match your branding.

5. Add Form and CTAs: Include a lead capture form and compelling calls-to-action (CTAs) relevant to your campaign objectives.

6. Integrate with Tools: Connect your landing page with marketing tools, CRM systems, or email marketing services for seamless data integration.

7. Mobile Optimization: Ensure your landing page is optimized for mobile devices. Test and adjust elements to provide a smooth experience on various screen sizes.

8. A/B Testing: Set up A/B tests to experiment with different elements, such as headlines, images, or form placements, to identify the highest-converting variations.

9. Add Conversion Tracking: Implement conversion tracking to monitor and analyze the performance of your landing page in terms of lead generation or other goals.

10. Custom Scripts (if applicable): Include custom scripts or third-party integrations for additional functionalities or tracking.

11. SEO Settings: Optimize your landing page for search engines by adding meta tags, descriptions, and relevant keywords.

12. Preview and Test: Preview your landing page to ensure it looks and functions as intended. Test the form submission process to confirm data capture.

13. Set Up Variants (if applicable): Create multiple variants of your landing page to test different approaches and optimize for higher conversions.

14. Publish Landing Page: Once satisfied with the design and functionality, publish your landing page and make it live for your audience.

15. Analytics and Insights: Monitor landing page performance using Unbounce's analytics. Track key metrics like bounce rate, conversion rate, and user engagement.

By following these steps, you can effectively use Unbounce to create, test, and optimize landing pages for maximum conversion and engagement with your target audience.

52

16

Google Tag Manager (GTM) for managing website tags and tracking codes:

To use Google Tag Manager (GTM) for managing website tags and tracking codes:

1. Sign In or Create an Account: Access the Google Tag Manager platform using your Google account credentials. If you don't have an account, you can create one.

2. Create a New Container: After logging in, click on the "Create Account" button, and then create a new container. A container is a virtual space where you manage your tags for a specific website.

3. Set Up Container: Provide details such as the container name, target platform (Web, iOS, Android), and choose the relevant container settings. Click "Create."

4. Install GTM Code on Your Website: After creating the container, you'll be given a GTM code snippet. Add this snippet to every page of your website just after the opening `<body>` tag.

5. Preview Mode: Before deploying changes, use the "Preview" mode in GTM to see how your tags will behave on your site without affecting the live version.

6. Create Tags: Tags are snippets of code or tracking pixels. Create tags for various analytics tools (e.g., Google Analytics, Facebook Pixel) or other marketing tools.

7. Create Triggers: Triggers define when and where your tags should fire. Common triggers include pageviews, clicks, form submissions, etc.

8. Create Variables: Variables store dynamic values that can be used in tags and triggers. Set up variables for elements like page URLs, user IDs, or custom data.

9. Test Your Tags: Use the "Preview" mode to test your tags, triggers, and variables to ensure they work as expected on your live website.

10.Publish Changes: Once you've tested and verified that everything is working correctly in the "Preview" mode, publish your changes to make them live.

11. Version Control: Google Tag Manager provides version control, allowing you to roll back to previous versions if needed.

12. Debug Mode: Use the built-in debug mode to troubleshoot any issues and see which tags are firing on specific events.

13. Built-in Tags and Templates: Take advantage of GTM's built-in tags and templates for popular tools to simplify the setup process.

14. Collaborate with Teams: If working with a team, leverage user permissions in GTM to control who can make changes to your container.

15. Documentation and Learning: Explore Google Tag Manager's documentation and resources to deepen your understanding and make the most of its features.

By following these steps, you can effectively use Google Tag Manager to manage and deploy various tracking codes and marketing tags on your website efficiently.

17

Sprout Social for social media management and analytics:

To use Sprout Social for social media management and analytics:

1. Sign Up/Log In: Create a Sprout Social account or log in if you already have one.

2. Connect Social Media Accounts: After signing in, connect your social media accounts such as Facebook, Twitter, Instagram, LinkedIn, and others.

3. Dashboard Overview: Explore the Sprout Social dashboard to get an overview of your connected social media profiles, messages, and analytics.

4. Compose and Schedule Posts: Use the publishing tool to compose and schedule posts for multiple social media platforms. Plan your content calendar in advance.

5. Engagement and Monitoring: Monitor and engage with your audience by responding to comments, mentions, and direct messages directly from Sprout Social.

6. Social Listening: Utilize social listening features to track brand mentions, industry trends, and relevant keywords across social media.

7. Collaboration: If working with a team, collaborate by assigning tasks, responding to messages, and managing social media activities collaboratively.

8. Reporting and Analytics: Access Sprout Social's analytics to track the performance of your social media efforts. Measure engagement, follower growth, and other key metrics.

9. Task Assignment: Assign specific social media tasks to team members within Sprout Social for better workflow management.

10. Mobile App: Stay connected on the go with Sprout Social's mobile app, allowing you to manage and monitor your social media activities from your smartphone.

11. Social Media Calendar: Use the calendar view to visualize your scheduled posts and plan your content strategy effectively.

12. Keyword and Hashtag Tracking: Monitor the performance of specific keywords or hashtags to stay informed about relevant conversations in your industry.

13. Custom URL Tracking (if applicable): Utilize custom URL tracking to measure the effectiveness of your social media campaigns.

14. Customer Relationship Management (CRM) Integration (if applicable): Integrate Sprout Social with CRM tools for a more holistic view of customer interactions.

15. Educational Resources: Explore Sprout Social's educational resources, including webinars, guides, and articles, to enhance your social media management skills.

By incorporating these functionalities, you can effectively use Sprout Social as a comprehensive tool for social media management, engagement, and analytics.

18

Zapier for automating workflows and connecting apps:

To use Zapier for automating workflows and connecting apps:

1. Sign Up/Log In: Create a Zapier account or log in if you already have one.

2. Create a Zap: In Zapier, a "Zap" is an automated workflow between two or more apps. Click on "Make a Zap" to start creating your automation.

3. Choose a Trigger App: Select the app that will trigger the automation. This could be an event like a new email, form submission, or social media mention.

4. Connect Your Account: Connect your account for the chosen trigger app and set up any necessary permissions.

5. Set Up the Trigger: Configure the specific trigger event that will start the automation.

6. Choose an Action App: Select the app where you want the data to be sent or an action to be performed.

7. Connect Action App Account: Connect your account for the chosen action app and set up permissions.

8. Configure the Action: Define the specific action that should take place in the chosen app as a result of the trigger event.

9. Test the Zap: Before activating the Zap, test it to ensure that the trigger and action work seamlessly together.

10. Customize Data (if applicable): Modify and customize data mapping between trigger and action apps if needed.

11. Filter Conditions (if applicable): Set up filters to conditionally control when the Zap should run based on specific criteria.

12. Delay Actions (if applicable): Add delays to space out actions within the Zap, if necessary.

13. Multi-Step Zaps (if applicable): Create more complex workflows with multi-step Zaps by adding additional actions.

14.Activate the Zap: Once satisfied with the configuration and testing, activate the Zap to start the automation.

15. Monitor Zaps: Keep an eye on your active Zaps within the Zapier dashboard. Check for any errors or issues.

16. Explore Zapier Integrations: Explore Zapier's extensive library of integrations to discover new ways to automate tasks across various apps.

17. Organize Zaps with Folders (if applicable): If you have multiple Zaps, organize them into folders for better management.

18. Educational Resources: Take advantage of Zapier's learning resources, including documentation, webinars, and community forums.

By following these steps, you can effectively use Zapier to automate repetitive tasks and create seamless workflows between different applications without the need for manual intervention.

19

Grammarly for improving your writing and checking for grammatical errors:

To use Grammarly for improving your writing and checking for grammatical errors:

1. Sign Up/Log In: Create a Grammarly account or log in if you already have one.

2. Browser Extension: Install the Grammarly browser extension for your preferred web browser (Chrome, Firefox, Safari) for real-time writing assistance on websites.

3. Desktop App: Alternatively, download and install the Grammarly desktop app for offline writing assistance.

4. Browser Integration: If you use online platforms like Gmail, Google Docs, or Microsoft Office Online, Grammarly integrates with these tools. Enable the integration for in-context grammar checking.

5. Write or Paste Text: Start writing directly in the Grammarly Editor, paste your text, or begin composing in an integrated platform where Grammarly is active.

6. Real-Time Suggestions: As you write, Grammarly provides real-time suggestions for grammar, spelling, punctuation, and style improvements. Suggestions appear underlined with a color-coded system.

7. Accept or Ignore Suggestions: Review Grammarly's suggestions and choose to accept or ignore each recommendation based on your writing style and intent.

8. Style and Tone Recommendations: Grammarly offers insights into your writing style, tone, and readability. Adjust your writing style goals based on the context of your content.

9. Plagiarism Checker (Premium): If you have a Grammarly Premium subscription, utilize the plagiarism checker to ensure your content is original.

10. Vocabulary Enhancement: Grammarly suggests alternative words and phrases to enhance your vocabulary and improve the overall quality of your writing.

11. Set Writing Goals: Specify your writing goals, such as audience, formality, and intent, to receive tailored suggestions that align with your objectives.

12. Document Type (Premium): Grammarly Premium allows you to choose specific document types, such as academic, business, or creative, for more accurate suggestions.

13. Download Browser Extension for Microsoft Edge or Safari (if applicable): Install Grammarly extensions for Microsoft Edge or Safari if you're using these browsers.

14. Weekly Writing Stats (Premium): Track your writing progress with Grammarly's weekly writing stats, including word count, productivity, and vocabulary usage (available in Premium).

15. Grammarly Mobile Keyboard (if applicable): Install the Grammarly keyboard on your mobile device for writing assistance while typing messages or emails.

By following these steps, you can effectively use Grammarly to enhance your writing, improve grammar and style, and ensure that your content is clear, concise, and error-free.

68

20

ConvertKit for email marketing and automation:

To use ConvertKit for email marketing and automation:

1. Sign Up/Log In: Create a ConvertKit account or log in if you already have one.

2.Dashboard Overview: Upon logging in, explore the ConvertKit dashboard, which provides an overview of your subscribers, forms, sequences, and broadcasts.

3. Create a Form: Start by creating a sign-up form to collect email addresses. Go to "Forms" and create a new form. Customize the form fields and design to match your brand.

4. Integrate Forms on Your Website: Embed the form on your website or use ConvertKit's landing pages to capture subscriber information.

5. Create a Sequence: Sequences are automated email series. Go to "Sequences" and create a new sequence. Set up emails, delays, and triggers to automate your email communication.

6. Broadcasts (One-Time Emails): Create one-time emails known as broadcasts to send time-sensitive content, announcements, or newsletters. Go to "Broadcasts" to create a new email.

7. Segmentation: Use tags and segments to organize and categorize your subscribers based on their interests, behavior, or other criteria.

8. Automation Rules: Set up automation rules to automatically tag or move subscribers between segments based on their interactions with your emails or forms.

9. Subscriber Management: Manage your subscribers by viewing their details, adding tags, and manually segmenting them if needed.

10. Integrate External Services: Connect ConvertKit with other tools and services you use, such as your website, e-commerce platform, or CRM, to streamline data flow.

11. Reporting and Analytics: Monitor the performance of your email campaigns, forms, and sequences using ConvertKit's reporting tools. Track open rates, click-through rates, and subscriber growth.

12. Custom Branding: Customize the look and feel of your emails to match your brand by using ConvertKit's email editor.

13. RSS Campaigns: Automate email updates by setting up RSS campaigns to send your latest blog posts or content to your subscribers.

14. A/B Testing (if applicable): For ConvertKit Pro users, conduct A/B tests on your subject lines to optimize email open rates.

15. Learning Resources: Explore ConvertKit's educational resources, including tutorials and guides, to enhance your email marketing skills.

16. Integrations: Take advantage of ConvertKit's integrations with other tools and platforms to extend its functionality.

17. ConvertKit Community: Join the ConvertKit community to connect with other users, share insights, and seek advice.

By following these steps, you can effectively use ConvertKit to build and nurture your email list, automate your email marketing campaigns, and engage with your audience.